SUICIDE HOTLINE HOLD MUSIC

SUICIDE HOTLINE HOLD MUSIC

POEMS

JESSY RANDALL

 RED HEN PRESS | PASADENA, CA

Book design & layout by Latina Vidolova & Selena Trager

Library of Congress Cataloging-in-Publication Data

Names: Randall, Jessy, author.
Title: Suicide hotline hold music : poems / Jessy Randall.
Description: Pasadena, CA : Red Hen Press, 2016.
Identifiers: LCCN 2015050371 | ISBN 9781597097260 (paperback)
Subjects: | BISAC: POETRY / General.
Classification: LCC PS3618.A625 A6 2016 | DDC 811/.6—dc23
LC record available at http://lccn.loc.gov/2015050371

The National Endowment for the Arts, the Los Angeles County Arts Commission,
the Los Angeles Department of Cultural Affairs, the Dwight Stuart Youth Fund, the
Pasadena Arts & Culture Commission and the City of Pasadena Cultural Affairs
Division, the Ahmanson Foundation, and Sony Pictures Entertainment partially
support Red Hen Press.

First Edition
Published by Red Hen Press
www.redhen.org

ACKNOWLEDGMENTS

Versions of some of these poems and comics first appeared in *Arsenic Lobster, Asimov's, Bat Terrier, Eclectica, Escape into Life, FemGeniuses, Flywheel, Josephine Quarterly, Knee-Jerk, Lily, McSweeney's, Menacing Hedge, The Mom Egg, Mountain Gazette, No Tell Motel, On Barcelona, Opium, Oracle, Rattle, Red Lightbulbs, Red River Review, Scud, Snakeskin, Spiral Orb, Star*Line, Strange Horizons, Sugar House Review, Thirteen Myna Birds, Tilt-a-Whirl, Toad, Toucan, Umbrella,* and *West Wind.*

for Ross
you are my love

CONTENTS

SUICIDE HOTLINE HOLD MUSIC

We play cheerful music on the suicide hotline—
cheerful but not *too* cheerful.
Nothing with lyrics.

Sometimes, when I finally talk to them,
they're crying, and sometimes they keep crying.
I fight the urge to tell them jokes.

Sometimes they get on my nerves.

Sometimes I ask them to see things from my point of view.
They gulp. They try. Even in crisis
they are polite.

I ask them where it hurts.
They always have an answer.

Here's what they don't know. When I play the music,
I'm still on the line. I listen to them breathing.
If their breathing slows, I keep playing
the hold music. I'm like a deejay and I'm like
a doctor. I adjust the music with care. I fine-tune,
giving them what they need at just that moment.

I'll ask them to hold and play the music again.
I have a button I can press that makes the music skip.
The same sound repeats for twenty seconds.
When I get back on the line with them, they never fail
to let me know about the problem. They're helpful.
"Thank you," I say. "We'll fix that for next time."

It reminds them they are part of the world. Then
they tell me things, sometimes haltingly,
sometimes in one big rush. How they feel,
how bad it is.

I can keep them on the line for hours.

The main thing is to keep them on the line.

PUBLIC SERVICE ANNOUNCEMENTS

1. Get Well Soon
2. Have a Nice Day
3. Sweet Dreams
4. I Love You
5. Have You Lost Weight?
6. Hello

THE PRECISE INSTANT I BECAME A TEENAGER

was when I realized I wanted to drink your backwash.

I mean at first I thought, if we could
share a soda, I wouldn't mind your germs,
I wouldn't even mind your backwash.

And then,

I mean then,

I realized I actually
wanted your backwash.

I wanted soda that had been in your mouth
to be in my mouth.

It wasn't mature like the opposite of immature.
It was mature like "for mature audiences only."

VALENTINE

I'm thrown at you like
a bean bag in a carnival game.

I send you a valentine with a picture
of a *Temple of Doom* barbarian
pulling out a man's heart.

You send me a valentine
raked with Catwoman's claws.

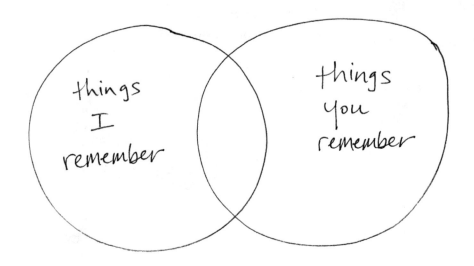

things I remember

things you remember

my
advice
to
you

what
you're
actually
going
to do

AMIR'S FALAFEL

Two years after
I moved out of New York
and practically forgot
everything about
the entire city,
I went back to Amir's on 114th Street.

"The usual?"
said the guy behind the counter.

THE WAVE OF PANTSING

The wave of pantsing swept down the hall,
flooding the small spaces between lockers,
the thin cracks in the concrete floor.

Boys ran, clutched waistbands,
squatted defensively. They knew.
They understood the power of pantsing.

Girls were automatically safe. They had
other terrors. The wave of pantsing was only
a wavelength of light, for them. It didn't hurt.

It wasn't the first wave. Others had brought
the school to its knees. Chinese jump rope.
Friendship pins. Folded paper that told the future,

or told who you really were, or whom
you really loved. We foretold riches or misery
based on a code of letters and numbers.

But no one could have predicted, shack
or mansion, the pantsing. The pants
brought low. Not removed—no—that

would be too dignified. Michelangelo's David
wore no pants, and he looked good. But never
has sculptor—nor, for that matter, poet—

attempted this impossibility, to surf atop
the wave of pantsing and not land rough,
neither pantser nor pantsed, aloof, above.

But what is he thinking, the person being pantsed?
Let it end? Am I zitted? How long must this go on?
The humiliation: he finds himself praying, age thirteen,

entering an unreal world. But what
does he pray? He doesn't even know.
That his closed eyes will protect him.

That twenty years from now no one standing, staring,
will remember. But he will remember. He doesn't think
to pray that he won't.

Was the wave one-time, or will it repeat?
Is *pantsing* still a word? Maybe this is why
we have children: to put them through it, to find out.

EVERYONE'S HAIR IN MIDDLE SCHOOL

Alan's hair was like *peeyome! peeyome!*
Dan's hair was like *fshhhh.*
My hair was like *mmmleeyeh.*
Amy's hair was like *shooom.*
Grace's hair was like *beedlybeedlybeedly.*
Suzie's hair was like *schlyooosch.*
Mr. Fraction's hair was like *POING!*
Mrs. Donahue's hair was like *chhhhhh.*
Sarah's hair was like *kuh-SHAH.*
Karen's hair was like *frukk.*
Ross's hair was like *foozh!*

distance from your house to my house

distance from my house to your house

POETRY COMIC FOR THE FARSIGHTED

A RUSSIAN POLICEMAN MAKES ME THINK OF YOU

When someone asks me what day it is
I think of you, and also a Russian policeman
makes me think of you, or the Russian
word for policeman, actually, which is
a word I only think of *after* I think
of you, so perhaps I should say that
you make me think of a Russian policeman,
or the word for it, anyway, with its letters
like connecting spikes and no way to tell
where one letter ends and another begins.

WE ALL FALL

We all fall
down.
We don't all fall
well.

When you throw
the chain on your bike
(and you will), don't fight
the fall. Fall with aplomb.
Just succumb. Let your body
drift to the ground,
falling where it may.
Because it will anyway.

When you're thrown over
by a lover (and you will be,
over and over), fall and feel
as blue as blue.
But you're still you.
We can't be pushed into love,
but we can be pushed out.
Only love can break your heart.

SPONTANEOUS

So what if I'm not
very spontaneous?
And anyway I could be
if I wanted to.
I could just up and . . .
well, no, I couldn't.
I can't even
think of anything.

THE POMEGRANATE SEED DISPUTE

She said you eat the whole thing.
She learned it in college.
Not the whole fruit, but the whole seed.

He said you suck out the juice and spit out the seed.
Or you'll be sick. He acted like he knew.
Like he'd been doing it his whole life.

But I learned it from a *professor*, she said.
It's not the sort of thing you can learn, he said.

questions
I
ask
you

answers

you

give

me

2

candy box of boyfriends

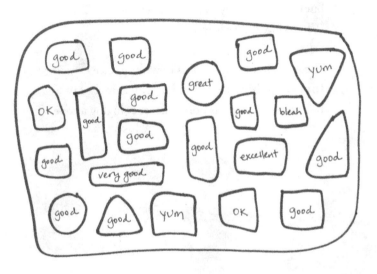

A DIFFERENT KIND OF STUPID

Rapunzel never compared the weight
of the witch and the prince. How dumb,
if she did. No, she was pregnant,
that's how the witch knew.

So, a different kind of stupid, up there
in her tower. You could argue
she loved him, and sure, she may have,
but he was the only man she'd ever met.
What kind of love is that?

The stupidest thing of all is how the prince
left her up there, day after day. Some might say
he knew what he was doing, never bringing a rope.

YOU KNOW THAT SONG

You know that song—what's the name of that song, the one that goes *something something, something something something, something . . .*

You mean the one that goes *something something something something something something?*

No, it's *something something something, something something something, something something something.* Do you know that one?

AT THE KENNETH KOCH WEDDING

"You were wearing your Edgar Allan Poe printed cotton blouse . . ."
—Kenneth Koch, "You Were Wearing"

The groom sits in the Kenneth Koch hammock
while the bride slides into her Alexander Calder dress.
For two years they have been using e.e. cummings birth control,
slipping only once on the Diane di Prima banana peel
and falling into the Nikki Giovanni fountain.
"Do you love me?" asks the Frank O'Hara bride.
"More than anything," answers the Frank O'Hara groom.

Fifty years later, at the Philly Jo Jones funeral,
the one left living cries 200 Robert Rauschenberg tears.

LOVE IS

"Love is patient, love is kind and is not jealous; love does not brag and is not arrogant."
—1 Corinthians 13:4

Love won't throw up all over you. Love is nice! Love is not an annoying fat man sitting next to you on the plane eating beef jerky. Love is soft. Love is warm. Love is furry, et cetera. Love is the smell of bacon frying, if you like bacon, which not everyone does, but most people do. Love is not an idiotic computer game. But let us not speak of what love is not, for then we will be here all day, and love is patient, but not that patient.

My Ability to Make a Clear Graph

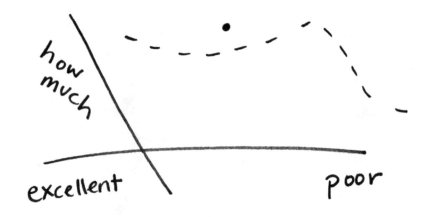

how
much

excellent

poor

Origami Koala Instructions

1. Fold this sheet on the dotted line

- - - - - - - - - -

2. Now you can't see the instructions any more.

HOW I LOVE PARIS

How I love Paris, Paris in the springtime, or even with sludge, and all because of you, because of you not being there. You don't live in Paris.

How I love Google, genius-like Google, it's brilliant and fast—how I love Google, and all because of you, because I never find you via Google, you're invisible on the Internet, it knows nothing about you, no marriage, no success, you're not even listed as competing in a 5K run.

How I love the universe, the glorious, enormous universe, it's so infinite that a fraction like you can be forgotten, discounted, you're astronomically small in the universe.

And how I hate falling asleep at night and dreaming, and you can see why.

IS IT OKAY TO CRY AT WORK?

Today we're asking people, Is it okay to cry at work? Let's see what this person thinks. This person thinks you should not cry at work. This other person thinks it's all right. This other person thinks you should cry all the time no matter where you are. This other person thinks that you should try to make other people cry whenever possible. This one can't answer, she's crying so hard.

ATARI CENTIPEDE

I'm breaking apart frantically
I'm falling so fast
I'm falling faster and faster
That's normal, right?
They try to stop me
They want to be the ones to kill me instead of me.
They want to hit every part of my body with their guns.
They think it's fun.
Meanwhile my body begins to block me.
My own body my enemy now.

WHAT WOMEN WANT

We want the breath you used
to blow up that balloon.

But we don't want you
to pop the balloon.

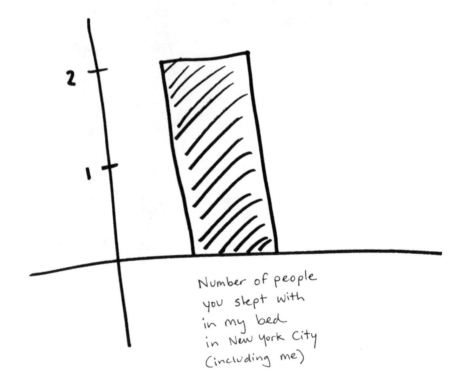

Number of people
you slept with
in my bed
in New York City
(including me)

you, to me   me, to you

DREAMS I HAVE HAD ABOUT SPIKE FROM *BUFFY THE VAMPIRE SLAYER*

I am Buffy's friend, and I like Spike, but he likes Buffy.
I am Buffy, and Spike and I are in love.
I am Buffy's friend, and Spike and I are having a secret affair and we can't tell Buffy.
I am myself, and Spike loves me and not Buffy.
I am myself, and Spike loves me, but I tell him I am married with two children and can't be with him.
I am myself, and I know I am married with two children, but I know this is a dream, so I can be with Spike.
Spike and I go to the Metropolitan Museum of Art.
Spike and I have an inside joke about the song "That's the way, uh huh uh huh, I like it."
I understand Spike in a way that Buffy never could. We have a long history together. We have been through so much.
I am amused to find out that Spike will be hosting a best-hits Buffy clip show. I can't wait to tease him about it.
The more dreams I have about Spike, the more I am likely to have. The dreams do not forget each other. They are connected, like book chapters. Sometimes I wake up from a Spike dream and remember other dreams from other nights, dreams I have not remembered before.
I feel like I should not even write these things down, because my relationship with Spike is private.

VOICES FROM THE PAST

are everywhere. On the subway
one tells me to stand clear
of the closing doors. At home,
another tells me I have two
telephone messages waiting.
As with any voice from the past,
I can't answer back. We're ghosts.

YOUR GLOW-IN-THE-DARK HEART

I can see your glow-in-the-dark heart
from halfway across the room
and it isn't even dark.

TEN THOUSAND BOOKS

These books are
holding up the house.
Or holding it down.

They have weight,
like all the degrees
of a family.

They are
wonderful
and horrible.

They are kept in a room
like hats and shoes.

They look
good on you.
They change you.

I guess it depends
on whether you think
your brain keeps you
on the ground
or defies gravity.

fuck you fuck
you fuck you
fuck you fu
cky
ou f
uck
you
fuck you fuck
you fuck you f

ucky
ou fu
ckyo
u fu
k you
fuck
you fuck
you fuck

you
fucky
ou fuck
you fu
ck yo
uf uc
k youfuck
you

fuck you uck you
fuc kyou fuck you
fv ck fu
youfv ck you
cky fuck y
ou ou
f fu
ck you
fuck you

fuck you
fuc kyo uck
uf uc youf
k y ucky
ou ou
fu ck
ck uf
yo kyouf
uf uck

yo uf
uc ky
ou fu
ck yo
fuck
you

48

I love you I
love you I lov
e you I love y
ou I lo
ve you
I love you I
love you I l
ove you
I lov
e you
I lov

e y
ou I you
love I lo
you ve y
I lo ou I
ve y love
ou I love y
ou love yo
u I love
you I l
ove

I lov
e you I
love yo
u I
lo
ve I
you I lov
e you I
love you
I lo

ve y you I
ou I love yo
love u I l
ove you I
love y
ou I
love I
you love
I lo you
vey I lo
ou

ve y love
ou I you I I l
love you I ove y
love y vey ou
ou I I lo ve
lov you I love
e y you I lo
ou ve yo

u I I l
love ove
you you
I lo ve
you I lo
ve you I
love y
ou

49

EUPHORIA OR A DEPRESSING OUTLOOK

My magic eight ball
offers euphoria or a depressing outlook
when I ask the same question
multiple times.

Which one is it, magic eight ball?
I'll just ask twice more.

TAXES

You showed me how
at the top of our taxes
there's a bold black box for
DECEASED.

They don't want you to miss it.
They don't want you to accidentally claim
your spouse is still around.

How we laughed.

But someday one of us
(only one)
will check that box.

BEST DAISY EVER

Petals reading: he loves me / he loves me / he loves me / he loves me / he loves me / he loves me / he loves me / he loves me

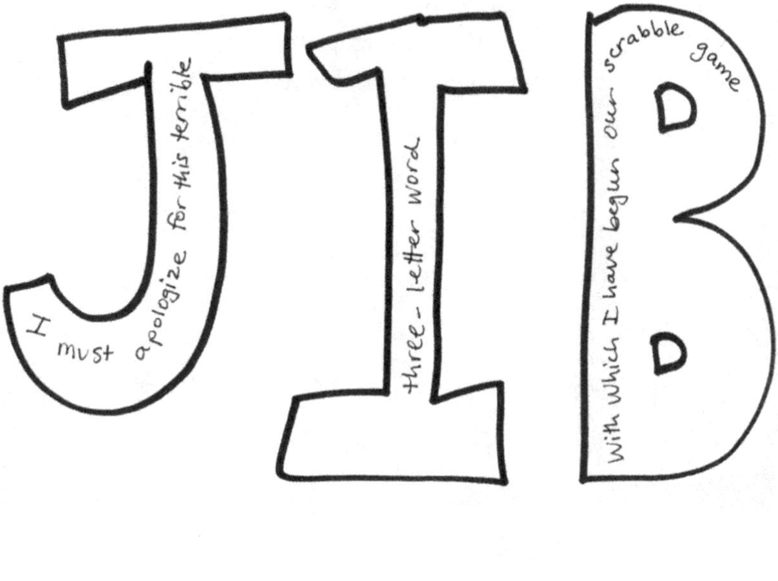
JIB
I must apologize for this terrible
three-letter word
with which I have begun our scrabble game

HUSBAND

You have disheveled
my sense of time. Now I'm
a puddle of goo, and you
are a hero sandwich. Or
we're in college. It's a collage
of love and craving. Let's go back
to the movie theater where
we put up the arm rest.
Every time you scrape the ice
off the windshield, I'm yours.

A QUESTION

I wonder what would happen
if I talked to my husband
the way I talk to my cat
sometimes.

For example, I could say,
"You are such a wonderful
husband husband husband!
How did you get to be
so wonderful? You don't even know,
you wonderful husband husband husband!"

Would anyone like that?

Very easy maze

me ============ you

Very easy matching quiz

you

me ⟋

Single-choice exam

1. I like

    ☒ you

2. You like

    ☒ me

TV Dinner of Love

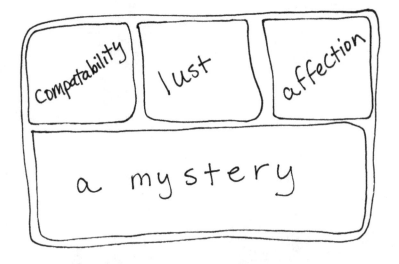

Compatability · lust · affection

a mystery

THE GIRLFRIEND OF TIME

"I'll always be there for you," said Time.
What a liar. Soon enough I got
"It's not you, it's me," and "Hey, don't take it
personal." "We'll tell everyone our break-up
was mutual," Time said, and I was left there,
dust suspended in jelly, a face full
of ectoplasm and no one to cry to.

CRACKLING OCTOPUS

(a found poem)

Whirlwinds. Snakes. Dominators. Lost empire fountain. Neon crash fountain.
Molten madness. Mammoth strobe. Mammoth brocade. Giant willow with
color tips. American thunder cake. Haunted fish. Crackling dragon Z shape.
Wave whistle. Clustering bee rocket. Total blast. The beast. Parachute battalion.
Rainbow fire. Dragon tears fountain. Red wave silver pony. Green glitter with
crackle. Crackling octopus. Howling wolf pack. Panoramic finale.

sources: online sales catalogs of US Fireworks, Half Price Fireworks, and Phantom Fireworks
(www.fireworks.biz, www.halfpricefireworks.com, www.fireworks.com)

THE PAPER COUNTRY

"I used to think all writers came from the same country."
—Kurt Vonnegut

In the paper country, letters of the alphabet
writhe on the sheets, flutter
from house to house. The natives
have gardens of pens, pencils,
typewriters on the vine, erasers are
snub-nosed roots like onions.
No one speaks here; there are only
the scratches and clicks and whirs
of the neighbors arguing, lovers' valentines,
the rendering of voices in a dream.

DREAM OF THE AVANT-GARDE

I dreamed they were writing
long articles about you,
you and your avant-gardeness.
I looked at the photos
and skimmed the text, hoping
for mention of me. Then wondered
what you were actually doing
that was so avant-garde, and
learned you were making words
out of dried beans on your hallway floor.
Brilliant! said everyone. Genius!
And I agreed, and we kissed
like middle-schoolers. And when I
told you about this dream, you said,
that's funny, I dreamed the same thing!

correct

incorrect/awesome

New from Narcissistic Sheep Comics...

POOL RULES

No smoking. No horseplay. There will be
no stealing of your best friend's boyfriend.
No nose-picking. Say please. In sexual matters,
be generous, but do not think of it that way.
No watch-wearing. No digital clocks. No
t-shirts with sayings on them. Spell *ketchup*
with a *k*. Do not drink to excess. If you must
read a book in the bathtub, be careful. Turn off
cell phones unless you enjoy subtle disdain.
No float-toys, no running, no communicable diseases.
People wearing cut-offs will be asked to leave.
No high-pitched squealing from those over two
years of age. Obey fire codes. If you can't sleep, turn off
the air conditioner, it might help. Cut sandwiches
into rectangles or triangles, either one. Shower first.

COMPETITIONS

(a collaboration with Daniel M. Shapiro)

We could put on mirrored sunglasses and have a staring contest. Or play a game that consists only of changing the rules. I would try not to win to make it last longer. We could introduce the world to the 104-sided die. The first to roll a prime number wins.

WHO WERE THOSE PEOPLE LAST NIGHT

They seemed normal
when they got into our bed

they were wearing normal things
and being normal

and then all of a sudden
their clothes were thrown
everywhere and they were

naked, performing bizarre,
outlandish acts upon each other

making a strange racket

and then in the morning
they got up and went to work
as though nothing had happened

THE WEIGHT, THE HEAT OF LOVE

The words slide down from their own weight,
like overburdened refrigerator magnets.
The explosions are adorable, like a gun
made of playdough. The mother laughs
at the bad word. The children don't know
the names of streets; their geography
works in a completely different way.
When they set up a store they don't know
the prices of things, so I make extravagant
purchases and clear the inventory. They are
so hot when they sleep, burning off all that love.

My Current Situation

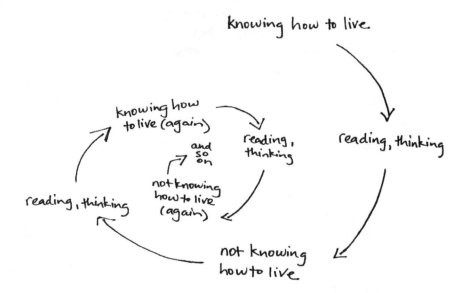

knowing how to live

reading, thinking

knowing how
to live (again)

reading,
thinking

and
so
on

not knowing
how to live
(again)

reading, thinking

not knowing
how to live

THE MOO OF THE DOOR

The floor sings. The door moos.
The bed flies up.
The farm is
so red, so plastic, it has
small pudgy pieces,
just right for my son's hands.

He pushes the animals
through the windows—
the horse, the sheep, the chicken
all piled into one room.

Then other toys go in:
a stuffed giraffe, blocks, a truck.

And then he puts his own feet
through the window, bends
his head over the other side,
embraces the farm like a body.

TOYS OF THE FUTURE

Cookie-Baking Gun
Fashion Mutant
Transgender Transformer
Camouflage Barbie
Pink Light Saber
My Little Robot Pony
Slinky

The baby has a slight fever.

HELMETS OF THE FUTURE

indoor helmet
outdoor helmet
driving helmet
swimming helmet
merry-go-round helmet

LOVE POEM FOR MY DAUGHTER

The way I love her is
completely crazy. It's unrequited.
Oh, I know she loves me—
but she doesn't love me *this* way,

the way I love her, which is
that I'm already angry,
F U R I O U S,
with people in the future
who don't love her enough.

Like I want to actually murder
these future people, commit violent,
bloody murder, with weapons,
or, if necessary, my bare hands.

IF YOU ARE EVER WONDERING

If you are ever wondering
what day it is
I'll tell you:

it's the day
you regret
not being nicer to your children

and it's the day
you think
you are too nice to them and
you're going to ruin them.

Also, it's the day
when you have to
clean out the cat box

BAD DREAM

He said, the letters of the alphabet
keep getting bigger. He said
his cup looked like a tank.
He was scared, he cried,
he threw up everywhere.

The next morning he didn't remember.
He felt fine. He got dressed,
played, ate a huge breakfast,
ran to school.

Meanwhile I'm still not recovered.
I can't recover from anything he does.
I still haven't recovered from just
having him.

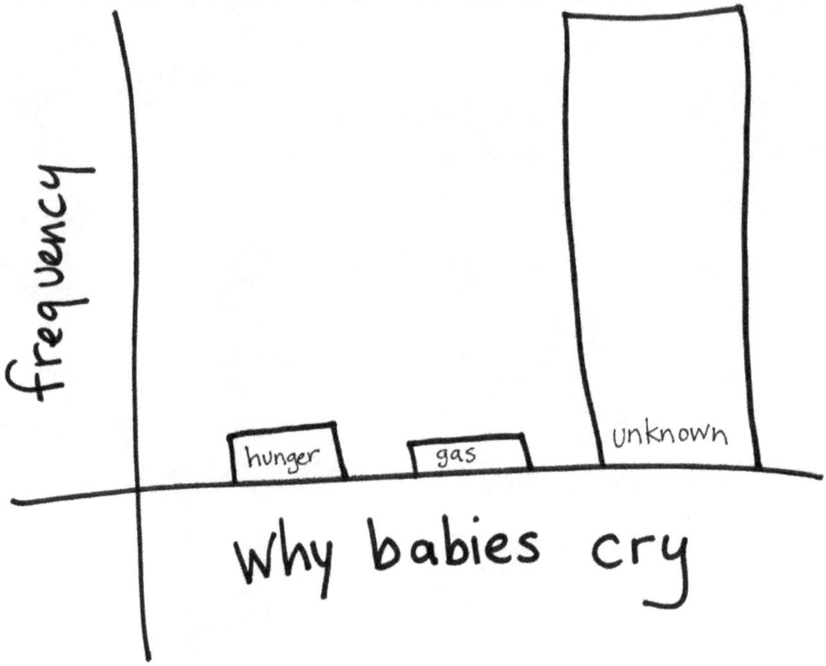
frequency
hunger
gas
unknown
Why babies cry

Nine Circles of Motherhood Hell

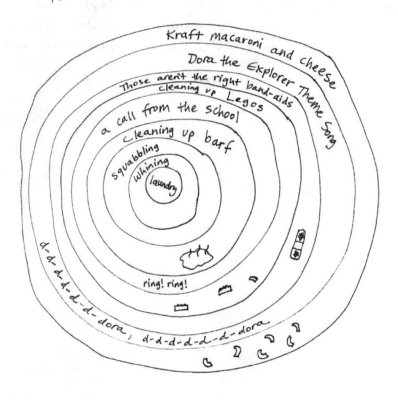

ONE HUNDRED THINGS

Some try to throw away one hundred things in one day and succeed. Some live in small apartments with purple bricks, or used to. Some gaze at their daughter curled up in a pink fur nest and almost perish from the plumpness of her sweet face. Some write appleappleapple over what they don't want you to read. Some forget all about the one hundred things, which is sort of like throwing them away but worse. Some draw one hundred things, rapidly. Today I brushed one hundred teeth, not all of them my own.

THE PRACTICE CHILDREN

*"Assignments might include divvying up responsibilities in a 'practice house' that
sometimes even included 'practice children' borrowed from local orphanages."*
—Emily McCombs, "Home Sweet Home Ec," *Bust*, August/September 2009.

We know we're only for practice. It's
a comfort to us. Nothing we do has any
long-term effect, so we can behave perfectly,
for a time, win prizes for our goodness and then
it's right back on the bus home again,
regular life waiting for us, the bunk beds,
the dinner trays, the horrible bathrooms.
We're practicing, too. We're practicing on you.

ON HAVING A DAY ALONE IN MY OWN HOUSE

I sculpt my gratitude into a Soviet-era monument, a giant blocky thing for the town square. Buses of tourists gawk at it, marveling at the effort. Mothers and fathers nod secretly to themselves: yes, for a day alone in my own house, I agree, such a massive thank you makes perfect sense.

I RUINED NEW YORK

I apologize. I'm the one who wrecked the feeling there, the alive, excited state of the streets, the way the museums embraced everyone who came in. What happened was, I was born, everyone liked me, I decided it was New York or nothing, arrived at eighteen, and then slowly over the next six years suburbanized first the entire Upper West Side, then Midtown, and eventually even the Village. Don't worry, though. I got my comeuppance. Look at me now, in Colorado, driving this gray car with the booster seat in the back. I can't even find it in the parking lot.

ON VACATION COMICS

Amount of things
I accomplished

Amount
I care

BATHING SUIT COMICS PRESENTS...
OPTICAL ILLUSION

is it a bikini? or is it...
A MONSTER?

ARE ALL OF THESE SHOVELS OUR SHOVELS?

At the beach we weigh the blanket down
with rocks and towels. As we read our books,
our plastic chairs sink deep into the sand.
Puzzles come together with slow exhilaration.
There's ice cream five minutes away.

We are not ourselves at the dinner table.
We are musical instruments, and animals,
and abstract ideas we can't explain.
Our children are like cousins.
They lock their doors, but we can still

get in. The gum they chew holds its flavor
for years. Their candy is antique. When they sleep,
their beds are still forts, and when they swim,
the ocean is still the ocean. If you want to know
whose shovels these are, just ask.

HOW MY ANATOMY HAS CHANGED

I no longer mind if you have other friends.
I don't need to convince you of everything.
You are a new kind of necessity—
less necessary but more important.
We are now the supervisors. My anatomy
has changed, drastically, but it's still
me in here. Once upon a time we wore
each other's clothes. Now we know
too much, not enough. The giant sculptures
of Wolfy's and Superdawg watch over
us and our children. Can their glowing eyes
offer protection? Will the octopus show itself?
It will, and you'll be by my side, or at least
in the same building.

TALKING ON WALKIE-TALKIES

Are you there Mom?
You forgot to say over.
Over.
Yes I am over.
Can you hear me? . . . Over?
I can hear you! Over.
I'm up in the attic over!
That's amazing over!
I'm coming down now over.
Okay over.

I HAVE NEVER GONE BACK TO NORMAL

after having children, but then,
I have to wonder, when exactly
was I normal? When
did everything change? Pregnant,
not normal. Newly married, no.
Waking up in Philadelphia in tears,
that wasn't normal. Though
I did get used to it. On Saturdays,
walking and walking and walking
from one library to another,
how can that
now seem normal?

FOOD DIARY OF GARK THE TROLL

Monday

breakfast: 70 boxes granola (no raisins)
lunch: 35 chickens
snack: 1 small child
dinner: 40 chickens

Tuesday

breakfast: 40 boxes granola (no raisins), 15 gallons yogurt
snack: 5 chickens
lunch: 2 ½ people
snack: ½ person
dinner: 42 chickens

Wednesday

breakfast: 55 boxes granola (with raisins)
lunch: 12 goats
dinner: 3 people
snack: 1 baby

WE ARE THE LUNCH-MAKERS

What is so awful about
making the child's school lunch?

Is it the dirtiness of the lunch box,
stained with lunches of the past?

Perhaps it's the smell of tomorrow's lunch
after today's dinner. To touch
the ham, the turkey, to breathe in
the peanut butter, the sticky sweet
banana, while not hungry at all.

To wonder about the pea pods.
Does anyone eat the pea pods?

It's so quiet, making lunch. The lunch-maker
has no choice but to contemplate
the meaning of the lunch, its inherent
disappointment, its endlessness. The
impossibility of making a lunch that's
everything to everyone: healthy and
delicious, comforting and a surprise.

The lunch-maker cheers herself up
by placing a leftover fortune cookie
in the lunch.

Let the lunch-eater interpret the fortune
any way she likes. It's her future.

AMBIGUOUS INSTRUCTIONS

"Everyone is special,"
is what they tell you.
"Be yourself—but not too much."
If you think about it,

is what they tell you
what you should believe?
If you think about it,
it gets complicated.

What you should believe
you have to figure out.
It gets complicated,
living in the world.

You have to figure out
all life's ambiguous instructions.
Living in the world?
It's almost impossible to!

All life is ambiguous instructions.
Everyone is special?
It's almost impossible to
be yourself. But not too much.

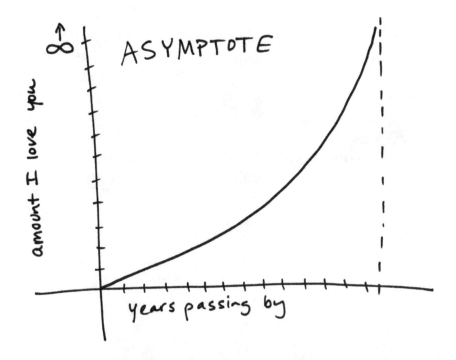

BIOGRAPHICAL NOTE

Jessy Randall's poems, poetry comics, diagram poems, and other things have appeared in *Asimov's*, *McSweeney's*, *Rattle*, and *The Best American Experimental Writing 2015*. Her first collection, *A Day in Boyland*, was a finalist for the Colorado Book Award; a poem from her second collection, *Injecting Dreams into Cows*, was featured on a street-cleaning truck at the Sydney Writers' Festival. She is the Curator of Special Collections at Colorado College, where she teaches a course in the history and future of reading.